TERMITES AMIDST THE MILKY WAY

(TURN TOWARD, TURN AWAY)

A COLLAGE BY CAROLYN SRYGLEY-MOORE

Kung Fu Treachery Press
Rancho Cucamonga, CA

Copyright © Carolyn Srygley-Moore, 2022

First Edition: 1 3 5 7 9 10 8 6 4 2

ISBN: 978-1-958182-25-3

LCCN: 2022949025

Author photo: James Srygley-Moore

Cover image: Jon Lee Grafton

Title page image of termite's nest by David Cardova, biologist

"I have enjoyed the work of Carolyn Srygley-Moore (aka C Leigh Srygley) for some time now, so I am pleased to write a few words about their new book, *Termites Amidst the Milky Way*, due to be released late November 2022. Throughout this new collection you will find C Leigh Srygley in firm control as each poem challenges us with complexity in form, rhythm, and content. What we may have considered the commonplace – matchbox toys, dolls, bicycles, bridges, house chores, sea shells, etc are used to bring us to an unavoidable truth – that now war, violence and terror have become the commonplace of our every day. C Leigh Srygley brings us to these conclusions over and over again through their firm control of context and form. With each read there is something new revealed, something proving that it was futile to think we could anticipate the next twist in the tale. These are poems to be savored and enjoyed for their composition, while the content makes us realize that C Leigh Srygley's dedication "to all resistance to tyranny and to those now living in a state of terror" is in some way applicable to us all. C Leigh Srygley: The only writer I know who can hang your tongue on barbed wire and have you wanting more.

> – PD Lyons winner 2019 erbacce-press International Poetry Prize.

"The work of Carolyn Srygley-Moore (a.k.a. C Leigh Srygley) is always essential, unique and revelatory, touching on the things that need to be touched on with a deft hand and a keen observational aptitude. Though I have been a fan of her poetry for many years, I consider this new book, an emotionally powerful poem sequence written in response to the current moral and humanitarian tragedy in Ukraine, her best yet. I heartily recommend it."

> —John Burroughs, U.S. National Beat Poet Laureate and author of *Rattle and Numb: Selected and New Poems*.

"Carolyn Srygley has always been a storyteller whose tales emerge from path and present, often at once, changing shapes like clouds change. She bonds the dream imagery of an Andre Breton with the moral witness of a Czeslaw Milosz - her two luminous masters - to haunt the careful reader with a perfect haunt."

-Allen Parmenter, Poet, Activist, Recovery

"Only forgetting can make something truly dead so to make it live on it must be written. Carolyn Srygley - Moore (AKA C Leigh Srygley) shapes her words in her mind which manifest on paper painting a vivid portrait. Her personal life intertwining with universal life to become art which resonates with her readers and captures our imagination. Perhaps Carolyn realizes and acknowledges her beliefs in the writing of poetry. Still, the poems don't leave us feeling overwhelmed but somehow hopeful and optimistic with strength to carry on and make the world a better place."

-Becky Farrell, Artist. Respiratory Therapist

Acknowledgments:

The late Mrs Jane Ambrose Srygley, my stepmom; a model
of what is good in us. RIP Southern lady, may you be
    forever well remembered

"J", of Kung Fu Treachery Press, fo Making this book
happen —: & for collaboration in layout & editing
    a vision never stated but understood.

Eva Srygley & dad, Bubba, actors in "Catching the Milky
Way — taking photos of the Milky Way one cold Montana
    November night

James, all the black coffee at the right moments at some
difficult hours & BYNX, my kid of love, tattoos & blue
calling me to stay in this world.

President Zelensky

The most Objective. Nuanced, & well presented news
Sources I can find. Great work for clarity amidst turmoil.

The animal rescuers of the Ukraine.
(Ben, Frankie, Piper. RIP)

My family as difficult as we are., have been.

Language, by which to confront
The disorder in & around us.

                              -Love, Carolyn

TABLE OF CONTENTS

What Would You Grab / 1

He Can See Birds / 2

These Are Our Private Wars / 4

What Is Cryptozoology / 6

Just Another Space Age Movie / 9

Wedding Flowers / 12

For The Vulnerable Ones / 16

Consequence / 18

The Yellow Bicycle / 20

Moon Bending / 21

Light Streaks Flash / 23

Pavarotti / 25

(A Barn Owl) Ventriloquism / 27

Shells Sea River Lake Sky / 28

Asking The Circus Actors / 30

As Fossils Stir / 32

Hematoma / 34

We Will Carry You (Acoustic) / 36

Without Borders / 39

The Suitcase // A Necessary Empathy / 41

Gaslight / 43

The Hunted the Hunt / 45

Eating Shrapnel Rainbows / 48

Heya / 49

Gripping the Porch Railing / 51

Perhaps / 53

Colonialism is / 55

Need / 56

Running out of Gas / 57

Wish She Had a Wand / 59 .

Staggers / 60

Formalized / 62

Hints / 64

These Are No Hamlets / 65

Erasure / 68

Linear Maybe / 72

Graffiti / 73

Binding (The Asteroid Rose / 75

Before / 77

After / 78

Lee Said To Me / 80

Glacial Air Pockets Opening / 81

From What Tree / 83

Wicks Shifting // As He Speaks / 84

Catching the Milky Way //

   The liberation of Kherson / 86

To the Liberation of Kherson— November 11, 2022

Fans who've followed Carolyn Srygley-Moore know she was made for these times. It wasn't just her previous accuracy of describing battlefields from World Wars I and II and the intervening follies we never seemed to leave. It wasn't just her fearless gaze that never turns away, even as modern media warn of micro-triggers, clucking like a mother hen for viewers to stop with the Looky-Lou rubbernecking. It wasn't just her ability to channel the language of prophets, often with a brevity and directness that stops time. Many of Carolyn Srygley-Moore's previous poetry collections have demanded of the reader a fearlessness that is often hard for mere mortals to muster.

The Ukraine collection, however, is much more. While some poets shudder at topical poetry, worried that the sell-by date for poems to age well will pass very soon and that the righteous anger at injustice will become forced, Srygley-Moore naturally avoids this through her unique powers of observation. She strips the gauze away and slaps us awake from our Long Covid. We are there, shuffling papers in Kyiv. We see Thor's Hammer in the ascendance, apogee, and perigee of flight, we feel the blow without benefit of noise-cancellation headphones, we feel the aftershocks throb to our marrow. As peace talks stumble on oblivious to every new atrocity, little moles are popping up elsewhere on the rapidly deteriorating game board. Don't worry, Carolyn Srygley-Moore will stick around to document the aftermath. But she will also play the omniscient prophet, on the scene in time to watch every hammer fall.

- Loring Wirbel, *Star Wars: US Tools of Space Supremacy*

This book is dedicated to all resistance to tyranny.;
and to those now living in a state of terror.

And I can think only about the starry sky,
about the tall mounds of termites.

Czesław Milosz, *Song of a Citizen,*
Warsaw 1943

What would you grab

What would you grab if you were
Leaving your future?

A girl grabs a green satchel of colored
Pencils

Sharpens the stubs on the train

& gives them away like ribs to
Gnaw

Along the way

He Can See Birds

Never afraid of the Darkness
10 fingers 10 toes &
An affinity with water
Lo
    Are we // are we
     born privileged
Smirking into the kiss?

Homes unlike crushed bone.
    Crushed ether Suckled
Moon

     Blood raft marrow

Yet
    Not everyone
& nearly all
Places

Leaf crashes like chocolate wrapper
Like shells rattling
Tattling
     An inhuman conscience

Countering concrete. Kangaroo pockets
    Turned inside out
   Flip flop go the babies.

Henna red the hair
What is fact?

Loring says
We have many lives
As many lives as the lucky have soul
Mates—:

Many chances to return
Having learned
Ways to be
Better people

Or that brown cricket
In the kitchen corner
Chirping

& Captain X
He says
"Where there are gnats
I see birds."

So we garden our fear
Where the Cats walk

These are Our Private Wars

This is how we can interpret
　　//know //
What war

Is. Isolated in a toddler's terror
Racing a matchbox car along a gutter

Who is left fending
Like street dogs & cats
& displaced bears

Foraging
For edibles. These are our public wars

It's how we are taught what war is
Can be

　　Rag doll huddle under
A kitchen table
Parallel to metro rails. But
There is refuge

　　The sacred bower
The one who sings leaps to the cliff top
His voice tolling

Just where the lighthouse is

The television tower

God's telescope however secular

The cemetery remarking presence
If only through shimmer & echo —: 4 years
    Old

        -         I fell over a wall
Walking Pandora fell
Into the Susquehanna
    & a man
Blank eyed from the second word war
Reached & taught me safety

He switches to this
Blocked televised station
Over & again yet

What Is Cryptozoology

We found a bridge amidst many
Bridges   A few parents & children like
Driftwood on the banks.
Pebbles.   Scattered
& scattering

   Like ridged water wicking out
From skipped stones.

I make wishes
Wherever I can some call it praying

I call it cussing

""

                Who took your Safe Place
That tree rattling with cicadas
Over the peace
A nightly walk amongst the
Inner nave of tree rings
The Thing
Who
Entered life & removed the lilt cadenced
The lullaby

                I remember crickets

Clamoring like recessed childhood's
Face against the window

Mister Munch the Painter

""

We found a passage
Like an alleyway
Full of fruits & wings & wool cable
Sweaters lain on sills
To dry & whistle
        Fallen
Into the tracks
            /// what
Is cryptozoology///. Human

Beast
/// what is BigFoot///

""

Horizon the grown man —:
        He
Ducks his eyes into the nape
Of
Her neck
Your sweating he says he says
Hey

It's only pink

It's only a UFO

  He says hey
It's just like praying.   Eating
The UFO.   Cradling red lichen
Driftwood
Til it
       Roots. Damn

  Cuss it out

Yah.
BigFoot
& UFO

Just Another Space Age Movie

2009 nine

Drops
Pressure
Scans—// stare at the blue sconce
   Nearly an archetypal lantern.

I see a red line thin indicating shore
Eroded & flattened of dune.
   But the beached whale
Ribs
Resist due gravity.

   It's like this everywhere.
Birds alight.
Gulls dirty blonde
Acid rain.

      I cannot decipher the letters.
A hunchback language.
The beast the beast who is the beast.
Perhaps someone who sees
As I see.

Blank a blank
Newborn as in old age
Huddled.
      Cezanne
Toulouse

Light morphs
Breaks day to dusk

The O turns to Q.
R to L.

I have abandoned sense // not forsaken
Sensibility.

Cartographer
Where is your ink.
Your parchment indecipherable
Long ago
Long ago.

Torn as the Dead Sea scrolls — O dear

Kiev century 9
The cinematographer's 9, a movie:
The soul in
A burlap doll
Dystopian
Spark
Bandura.

(NINE
a movie 2009
Director Shane Acker
Tim Burton producer
Based on a graphic novel)

Pro Brecht Plum Tree

Wedding Flowers

In that room

Dull
Iron bars between ourselves & a roof
   Rife with the memory of rain

       We lay plums
On a white cloth

Red plums.

You counted them like coins
Into the flat
Of my palms

   & I mounded them
Into a large wooden salad bowl
    Countdown
One by one

The smooth surface
Counterbalanced
The red

Walkway

The rain, deep rusted
Blood.

         Butterflies then again
      Is it simply (the way it is)   11

Catacomb Speak

Used to be
We'd come here nights: she says
    Carry the infants
From intensive care
Like melting snow angels
Wired to the dying sun. Maybe
A sleepy sun.
Nights only.

So the thin mother
Speaks to Foreign correspondence
The Evening News.

Nights only
She says.
    Then the days the days.

People & their animals
Hounds snuffing at my infant's feet.
My infant too weak for clinging.
    She silent trembles]

I
        have seen puppies
Or elderly dogs
Weeping scratching biting their own tails

Like the snake
Symbol of carbon
The element

In clean antiseptic shelters.
Yet forced to eat their own shit

Howling above below around them.
Too they are aware.

""

But these people
Are laying out picnics!!
Pork fat
Bread

""

Speech slurred
Lullaby vanquished
Yet we know we know.

Over there// here

""""

Some girl plucks the violin

Over where the station

Seeks out

A little light midst sleep & snore.

She strums a chord

That gathers.

Gathers more. Quartet

Is summoned

Then orchestra

A pocket full of coins jangling

Is a makeshift

Tambourine.

""

    A peace correspondent

Comes up from

The catacombs. What else is that

The metro

A bomb shelter underground

Full of time

Full of futures put on hold?

A toddler flies a paper airplane.

Holt kneeling

    Exchanges

A moment

Cronkite all over again

Signing off

    With the assurance

Tomorrow will arrive //
Our star willl hail come morning.
""

Cronkite
"And that's the way it is"

For the Vulnerable Ones.

Growing up, a suburb in Pennsylvania (Russia overtook
a suburb today// shot a family trying to escape over
a broken bridge), the neighbor was Ingrid. She was a
friend of
My mother's. I was very
Young & she is a light
Gentle
In my memory.

She was an immigrant from Germany.
After Stalin "emancipated " the
Civilians she came to this country.
She also confessed the multiple
Gang rapes she & others endured
Under these soldiers. She was a young
Girl at the time.

I do not recall much about
Ingrid.
But like my mother who lost her parents
Young, she did not disparage
The good she was granted.

I imagine
        She &
mom gave eachother
Baby formula or a cup of sugar
If we ran
Out.

I don't know if she was able to bear children or not,
I remember no children. I remember no family. Just
Ingrid. Alone &
Kind.

Remember the vulnerable ones.
Bless.   They are the shine

Consequence

That apartment, the house painter
Spoke of Michelangelo.
   Bled the Sheetrock red.

 I fried russet potato & diced onion
Set kitchen flower
Curtains afire,

Walked to campus
    Met with the pastor
  Gave him a xerox of some poetry

Set in his country of faith.
Nicaraguan dolls
Filled
His bookshelves with first edition

King James
Or To Kill
     a Mockingbird?
  First edition, my heart:: consequence.

Perhaps this isn't my country.
But I own a quarter acre, tangential
   To the village square

Of lottery & guillotine

Pull a straw of any length

Pick a strawberry

   From the straw weave passed

& die. Or thrive. In this movie

People have many lives —: but the pastor

Said goodbye

   Innocuously & carried away

His images-/: South American

Middle Eastern

Conflicts

Incarnations

Boys standing on their classroom chairs

Calling out out

The enemy faced down

The enemy

Which was themselves.

The Yellow Bicycle

Taught how to pedal a bicycle
The principles of balance

The sensation
Of gazing into the belly of monster
Urban lake sea

Seeing
Pulled by vacuum truth
Of minefields in outer space

You resist.
Like a fisherman
Pulling a shark to deck

You hold your own.

Moon Bending

They say children can do it
Bend the moon
In accordance with apt
Visions

Only children
The homeless
& abandoned puppies know.

Sculptors must turn to
Shafted iron
Set under torch
To turn steel to light arc

But they who know
What it is to be ransacked —:

To have the sac newly
Bust & by the mother devoured
The umbilicus too
Torn
          Or the one
Who has no housing
Beyond the greater organ
That sloughs
& molts
& betrays

Know how to take
Shafts of moon yellow falling gently
Through the declination

Rock smoking rock

& make the optical
Illusion
So warm
So fetal
So responsible &
Real.

Light Streaks Flash

Spark

& what is a firework?

We would lie on a blue quilt patched
Bandaid faces
Backs pressed
Down down
Vertebrae link to gnarled root
Mud mud

& what is a damn root
Or a tree taken hostage
Or ceasefire deferred
 Plum tree flower
I'd rather speak of you

I hear my dead father
Whisper
Pick at the threaded rot of his suit

Look over your shoulder
(What is it // going out to see fireworks)

You have seen this before.

A cat scratches at

Yarn rot
In the barn
Indeed what is a child what
Is a leaf

What is a human being

     All fortune tellers turn
In their scarves
& wipe sweat
From
Our eyes.

It is time

Pavarotti

Sings in the shower & washes
The sea froth
    Lifts lifts the long white handkerchief
 & steps
Into loss &
Loves

Anyway. It is no game
For song or chess it is no game
    The forced vow
Of silence. Voice box broken by
  Kiosk vendors
Dogs
Or tenors.

     Kicked like cans
   Kicked like baubles
Kicked like soul
Bared
    Gutted operatic stage.

Of course
He is dead now.
  But a person is singing
    Signing
The depths of shatter
Void.

I see a bird.
I see in the rubble a yellow bird

Amidst
The hollow skulls

Both honor & sacrament.
Pavarotti sings.

(A Barn Owl) Ventriloquism

This challenges
Reality
  As I know it
Emergency flares dulled —;
The owl comes to me
Like a cicada
In the woodland arc above me.
  Touch my skull
He says
There is a lump
Over which bone is crumbling.

True. Disintegration is not
Death. How many
  Skulls pressed
To crumble
Like ancient cities
Theater & cinema
  Taken; formations
To which the surgeon lifts his butchery
& says
My dears
Who showed you
What peace is?

Nothing to be done
Says the owl
Hoarse as a morning black lake frog.

Shells Sea River Lake Sky

package of boot socks, our priority
Then dog biscuits
Some red grapes.
    All meant to halt the shells
Falling.

        Sometimes we turn away
From what we cannot change —:

    Always liked shells, hermit crab
Hollows lying on the beach
Beside the shell of a dolphin's leap.

I see things
Through the filter of what
I've known // a cloud. Its smokey
Musculature ruptured by they who
Prey.

        Of course
I am
Limited. I inherited tall
Brass scales
From grandfather
A Nashville judge, 1930s.
Upon each scale

        Shells from river

Lake
Sea.

The ear of an
Infant is a shell also. Pure
Pink pink —: what are
Those shapes

Streaking down in unfathomable nudity
Toward the nuclear
Plant? It too, only a shell

    & the plutonium it leaks
& leaks
    We nightmare
We turn away

Into
God's minimalist stance
As a
Man, blank faced
Grinds heel to out a cigarette
Ember
    Upon the conch of absolutes.
   Breath is no absolute. Breathing

You sling dog food
Into the cart. & we go onward.
On. Nibbling the yellow
    remnant stars.

Asking the Circus Actors

Maybe the face is a dirt spun leaf
Just as the sagging beams
Are wrecked by webbing
  No arachnid
   No fishermen
But a possessed monster
Somehow
Took control
Taking control
       & surely
Ceilings sag worldwide
Speckled by honest lies &
Hints
Of black mold
Stealing oxygen we
Need
       As a team
As the children need
& as I sweep the crates
& tidy the books
Heaped all over
   I talk to the dogs
& I talk too to any evil lurking
At anyone's sill
"I will get you my pretty"
     But ask the circus
Actor the hatted painted

Elephant:
Evil
& the desire to sell
    Fabricated chocolates
Are two things
Difficult to take down.

As Fossils Stir

I wake at two
Am
  For the sake
Of laughter induced like labor
& cream froth
Poured
Into my green tea.
   On
The board of cork pinned
Of daily routine
Doctor
  Appointments
An errand for medicine, food; luxurious.
That Halloween colored butterfly wing
  Science tore
From the thorax
Stirs
A bit
   In the breeze. But blood is
Blood.

It is winter
Still. Infiltration
Memory
  The Prague
spring;
Eventual

Tanks

Crash in. Then.

Blood is blood still.

Shrill

The torn wing

Stirs, even

Lilts slightly. Undercurrents bear too

The hawk; or

A watermark

The vein of a leaf the rust

Vase of Athena underground

Stares.

Hematoma

The town square is a red moon
Reflected amongst ancient tombs.

They used to plan
City construction around graveyards;

Engraved stones of the dead
Newborns lean against the gutted

Cathedral walls.
This is not your god to which

I turn, uncertain
Even of the catacomb stench.

Once my husband & I
Dressed goth black & twirled black

Umbrellas the storm
Turned spoked & inside out

& we went sailing
Through sarcophagus walls

Like blasphemy; tank warplane piles
   Of burning diaries
Took to the granite

& imbued with loyalty

The dead stirred. Again: this is no

Worn out god

To which we could now turn.

We Will Carry You
(Acoustic)

Driving around
Thick licorice night
Ice laced puddles a hint of thaw

Driving
Seeking searching
That stained glass window

Lead traced fictions
Myths
Stubborn nonfiction. Driving

Folds unfolding the cloths yellow blue.
Baby baby I will carry you

Nobody hey nobody
Loaned me a space in a parking lot
To write & sketch

But I found this place
A refuge amidst speaking rubble & baby baby
I will carry you

Until home is home
Until you are back home again.

I have no feathered cartilage

On my back

Just sharp scapula jutting stubborn

& what if the angels are

Neither great nor small

But somewhere in between? Baby

Baby

    We will carry you

Your newborns attached to wires beep

Your elders in their narrow eyes

Yet even

They, they are somewhat surprised

& hey

    baby

    Walking toward that crowded train

Your dog your dog

Will lead you on

A pit bull will lead you on

Allowed on that whoosh feathered train

    Cause in that subzero

Lot

The call the call

It carries on & some window whispers

    Is that some unnamed

Deity or

Jesus moving amidst

The unhinged stained glass ruins

& fallen paintings dissent like dying

Lazarus

He saw the cusp

The butterfly mass like biting gnats

He turned back

Cause baby baby I

Have a need for God

    Some kayak riding deity

Suddenly

Today

        & little ones

We will carry you

Fog erasing borders scantily clad

The futures

    Padding like tiger boats

Baby babies young & old.

Without Borders

A train passed through
    along rims overgrown by yellow
flowers or wounds
  What's the difference;

Of an abandoned trestle
Just now
A trestle we were told was abandoned
    the train whooshes through

& I think
In the terrain
Uncharted of the Torn refuge just now trains
Sound out

The passengers & the freight
They carry

Sounding out
To they who conjure abandonment
When there is
None.

""

I always think of searches
  Do you

Amidst the heated whoosh
& crossroads
Of feral cats dodged & dodging pebbles
Skipped

& trains

  Canned peaches
Bust open
By rock & by hope
    A hunger raging

By food
Untamed //
    Coiling veins
Through fists & deciduous trees
& blue

    Those tree rings
Talking
Fusing
Fracture
        Bone
Touching
Marrow

      Without borders.

The Suitcase // A Necessary Empathy

It's cold but I'm not cold
I drag this red suitcase of voices around
   A camel's cargo
      A hump of old water.
Strange. I hear the degradation
The neighbor
    Her gossip hungry as street dogs
      In Brazil
& the pharmacist
   Discusses warplanes & technology
      The world lacked 100 years ago;
Sean says
It's a good thing, that lack. President
   Zelensky speaks to one ear
      With dignity begs in one ear —:
Step up
Civilization
   Step up! Putin rocks on his terrace
      Holding his face
As if he is his own lover
Rocks
      Like a savage horsefly burned
       Or Marc the dissociative
On a hospital smoking porch.
Well. At least I know I'm affected
   When girls at the office
     Gash slash my back;

Putin doesn't know
He just doesn't know
 Like

   Clown It
A monster dodging backyard clotheslines
Linen sheets hung
  By new refugees
    The mutter of silence
Cordons of mothers
"I must get my babies to safety"
  & God how I see the steps of
    Island constructs; hear
The erection of that statue
Eyes yes
    Face clearly defined
  By yellow moon suns O
The freed ones
  she has seen & been.

Gaslight

The gaslighter approaches
Crazy he says only crazy
He says.
    Limits define.

He is wearing a red polka dot bow tie.
    We are a little
Nuts I say; lose socks
Misplace winter
On blizzard days .

I know what coat & socks are for:

Not crazy

    & limits
Are no boomerang no rubber band
Snapping back to planes
Of corruption
Perversion
    The "Who deluded you" —;

    See it

A man stares down
A cordon of tanks /: don't know his name
Remember Tiananmen

Blurred of face on television
Video
      Photographs

   Seems not undone

Not blurred of aim.
   I hear Rain
The snowman is ice & kerosene
   Ripe with barb & Artemis arrow
A constellation cut of sky
An ideal
     Applied.

The Hunted the Hunt

Yellow orb

Night
Driving seeking an enclave
A bower of remembered lilac
There are only closed down
Shops like flooded waterfronts.

      I'd do anything
For them.//. He says.
    More than circle a square
A central
Town court
   Around which is built
A nave of lilac
Dismembered.

Hitler closed himself off in a bunker.
Putin speaks to two
    Listens to none.

//

I suppose on a very primitive
Level
     We recall the decency
In us. "I'm
Not surprised not remotely," they say

As the plant is ransacked
Plutonium residual in hazmat suits
Of skirt pockets

& intelligence is not only
Cognition. Once upon a time
Is revised
  From
That brutal nursery rhyme
Where even a giant peach
Is pixel with gruesome inhabitants.

That's not what I mean. Grappling
To dig the Baltics from packed
Ice. To cut its voluptuousness from
A parchment & place it
A yellow
  Carnation

Between pages of language
& crow feather
& a dictionary of trust

//

They say we have come too late.
I think that is the shock.
  Behind our televisions
Of graphic
Novels

We know it is no novel.
"I would do anything."
The angel's spine is prepared
To be ridden
    & our pilot warfare
Is our paper airplanes
If dissension //

   //

Absentminded eager reticent protest
Lapsing to & from in & out
Of what that decent
    Moon rising
Too didn't

Poe
       Die as a drunkard
  Stuffed like a scarecrow
With raven feathers
Because he had ideals.

(Inspired by dialogues

Eating Shrapnel Rainbows

Eating rainbows for breakfast
   We crouch in the hollow
Drumming our fingers
Even bored. Almost…

   Daddy said
In the Pacific Theatre
The Island of Okinawa
      They got sick of it

Nearly bored
The feel of guns
The pilot's stick

That strange flash of dream
   Like the
Tracks of a fleeing hare
They saw

Visit the faces of friends.
6 years killing
6 years nearly dead. He'd serve up
   Rainbows for breakfast
Syrup & butter
Fried green tomatoes & tea on the side.

Heya

Maybe there's nothing for us here
You & I

But a mutual familiarity with
The outhouse or moon cut

Against our palms
Passing along each other's faces.

I have no great words.
People like us focus upon

The ample bowl of summer
Plums even in dire weather. That

Definition of niched peach stone;
Still yesterday I sat through

The hurt of afternoon
With a woman. Her breathing rasped

Rang in the ears like an
Overdose & she was scared. Her eyes

Wide propped
By toothpick gods

Like eyes of shipwreck children
Underwater. Ah sure. Paintings

Or the wag of a griffin's face
Too make us breathless with beauty

Suspense
Horror
But
My friend's mother left
In sleep

There was no air. We are
Grounded to human consciousness by

That need to breathe. Underground
Metros play necessary currents

Air air
Necessity accordion lungs.

& thus we resist
& this we sing.

Gripping the Porch Railing

We are truly same
In the last encounter. Something
    Shifts a star lantern
Beyond the door
Though stars are fixed.
        It returns.
What I've read of the eclipse
The eclipsed. Not solar nor lunar
But a drone machination.
    They held to porches
They pressed face into shade
So silhouette could not
Betray.
         "I am not guilty."
     "I don't care."
As one body
One being
Fugitive false accuser tumble
Merged
    Into the waterfalls
Where good & evil
Not only coexist.
They are indistinguishable
They are one.
           But their
Grotesque copulation
Their stink of coupling

The fixed ideas of power
Shift as the North Star
Stays
                    The lighthouse
    Too
Refusing betrayal.

Perhaps

Perhaps it's a relief
To know heads of evil as
Unrecognizable

To the construct of your new world.
The podcasts
     Stagger reeling through

The fog.
Perhaps a release —: to know only
The language of body
Gesture

The full moon of love's voice.
She doesn't know
What I mean by /: rabbit /:
     But knows the fallibility of

Light. O the hidden
She says from gash spasm
Dream
     Roaches will be blasted
Bearing plutonium on their filth
Backs

She knows. Evil is evil
No matter what philosophers may say
At the border
  Feeding carrots
& winter fruit to the robot
Yet bleeding
    horses.

INVASION : colonialism is everywhere

Yet it is never justified.

Need

Ribs like eggshells
Soldiering pain from pain with
    Pain.
How imperative is it —:
To know the glacial
Air pockets
     Like shelters—: urgent
Bomb shelters —:

    A metro station too
A place to breathe.
  Huddled silence
Coaxing voice
From the crushed trachea
       Teacher

Teacher
    Spell out peace
Into God's naked promise
Raw
      Manmade
Black Mountain palm.

What does it hide
What remains hidden.

Running out of Gas

Picked up some apples the Lethe
   & drove on on
Highways of lions lapping blind milk
From hearts

I drove til
The gas tank
Was empty.

   I'm
Glad she's not living now
There are a few facts
   I'm glad death spared her
Shiny soul
The brim of a desolation
A discontent

That familiar winter.

   Indeed. I ran out of gas
Somewhere between convenience stores
Route 67. The nor'easter is coming.
My friend is feral
Or fetal
   & I too could scarcely rise
Today
For unlike the sun
     I have a semblance.

I have choice

Ducking my face into drifts

Oncoming. If I knew how to bear arms

If I wasn't considered crazy

 I'd cross the seas or drop

Drop

Via a parachute darkly winged

On those streets

 Built

In the Ninth century.

History is everything.

Naming is everything. The deer

Flashes her tail

& I am the consequence of

 What but the coupling

A man & woman

Who lived & dissented &

Carried arms

Piloted planes

Played nocturnals

 Keyboard dream Chopin.

Written

2/25/22

Date of full scale invasion begun.

Wish She Had a Wand

The blank
Of Merlin's face.
I hold his face
Cradle it
With hands & a trust
No longer possessed
& he splays
The fingers of hands
Ghost ghost
No longer controlled

Do we
Have I ever owned my hands
I / she says
& as she lunches
Mermaid sirens swirl

Merlin says: pile red
Plums
In glass punch bowls
Write a list
Things to be done or
Things
Errands
Pick up milk
Oil your engine
Measure willingness
Realize
The integrity of plums

Staggers

A gash in what is holy.
  Yet between the trees light peeks.
At once
            Capricious & precarious

Noon casts its
Shadows

  At the feet of deity Fatima
where it's said her tears appear to those

Prepared
Or not ready at all. To be human
    Is absurd

A crow an eagle
The wings of refuge & sanctuary
Clipped

A yellow parrot
        Stutters then speaks a humane
Coherence again. Patience

Of tree ring
Perhaps. Patient dusk rising
  Into the sloughing staggering dust.

Roadside casualties
Called into breath again. Bombs called
Back

Into the plane.

Formalized//

The straight face of assassin // how
   Many arsenic drops
Dropped into teacups? Tsardom attempted,
Reinvented—:

        Straight face, some virulent sitcom
Duplicitous
Comedian
Announces
Formally. Tanks not tea today. Wondering

    Does the shelling of civilians
Does carnage
Change The Leader's mind.
Any Leader.
        Challenging

Fences. Not Whitman but Frost. Students
Read sudden poems men &
    Women in cramped blue rooms at
The Y fresh from
Suicide & survivor catacombs
            Watch Prisoner cult clips
Spies, mandibular crunch,
The cyanide apple. Where
Are the children?

It's formal. Announced. Television
International.
Straight faced as the moon cast
Writing of Stonehenge—:
Ancient.
Cryptozoologies —:
   Air land sea
      Byrne sang
It. Always the water same same

Same
Passing through. Flares
Red refracted. Just passing through.

(For the people & government of
The Ukraine)

Hints

Well. Brain cancer got him.
That's what 96 year old Helen
    Said

About forms of death.
"Got him."

    My cousin died.
I don't know if it's like a drifting

Like suicide can be; is.
Entertaining consequence
    That you won't see —;

This is the
Beginning I told him. Isn't it.

Who is the last one standing?
The last wall

    When outer space
Is within us. A formidable

Solitude. Petals drop
Drop. It's something unreal. Arrogant.

Trying to control
Death. Head on.

These are No Hamlets

Soliloquies broken like thoughts
Scattered spore of dream
    A small cafe in Kiev
A couple is nibbling meat sandwiches
Not watching the news
Ignoring the news
        An infant sucks at a mother's
Terror a train station painted
Blue benches painted blue
The child pants he has such
Thirst
        A man
Unlike Hamlet
Does not query the absurdity
(It's an absurd time to be alive
Said Alex the student of zen
A few days ago
    As he ate cheese sandwiches
Like the passengers
Not yet having tumbled to Narnia)

I know little about zen
But those paintings of crossed black
Branches & plum flowers
Nor what zen has to do with
"The situation "
    (' who is
Number one")

But
Only the inhale & the
Big exhale

Exhume the coming ghosts
Or not ghosts
Yet

Breathe they say
Just act
& breathe

Surround sound
What is
A guerrilla
A coffee shop in Kiev

These hours aren't imagined. The sun
too over wounded land yet trees
Stand proud like lanterns. The snow
Dirty from months of y skinned truck
Exhaust collide against orange z & a
Diluted yet determined day. A displaced
Stag wanders into the parking lot then
Keen of scent leaps like the sudden. It
Is a morning drive peopled by a realized
Loneliness. It is matter of fact & without
Desperation. We each have our own
Pompeii the magma entering the birthday
Party captive. An ancient atom. An
Ancient burn, sudden, that fox seen
On a walk years ago, eye white combat
Eye white; each knowing, it was no game.
Perhaps
The name &
Place of wound —: the speaking of —;
Is no longer hidden
No longer forbidden.

Erasure

The necessity — instinct? —
    some feel to erase
Grind shoreline down.
Integrity
      Eroded
           even manatee
      no rock to measure
Self, experience.

""

How to Erase cultural
Identity
    A book of recipe :

Burning Koran Torah Bible
    Base // porn
Calling out the Jewish
The African
The queer

Whatever racket vise
   Bolted about their shine
   To blunt
   To render dull
    The exquisite.

Even books of blood

Ritual

Addressing the shapeshifters

Adolescent

—: a girl

       Outing powers of her won understanding

Teachers draw a sign pinned cork

& with a flashed palm

Or mechanical turtle

Proclaim won experience zero.

""

The Death Camps

Camps of internment

Spit

     the Irish the immigrant

   The refugees Palestine

Afghan

Rivers crossed in a deep

     Cultural hypothermia.

Ah freezing to death can be quick Painless. A man

Chanced upon in rusted gutted   Chassis

scattered with pills

     Or powder

Truly the memory of descent.

Ascent —

What has changed
But the target.
When the strike
            Loses its victim
It shifts to
        another.

Uvalde. Columbine Buffalo
Parkland Sandy Hook

She screams spits tears
The witness: one who ducked

Yet saw —: "you are Fraud."

""

I asked a man once —: do you think A person
imagines violation
Imagines rape.

        He responded
In grunt & platitude.
Only his thumb shifted.
A red squirrel took from a tree.

When target practice
Ends
    & the automatic
Is disappeared

The deer they say is no deer
      Of truth
But some
Irrelevant foam on sea glass
Ahistorical fabrication

      Globally
    Firebird will shake off erasure
As the golden hound shakes off water

    Shadow Light.   rise
Fist & a passage feather
Red cardinal
Blue crow
Foam crest of sea.

Linear Maybe

Down by round lake
Where solitary men paddle kayaks
    Linear as skipped stones
We park. I photograph grass
My silhouette
As sketched on blank paper taped
To a kitchen wall.
        Or watch Personas
Exchanged faces & vows
The dropped voice
The dropped soliloquy.

I sit in a parking lot.
I recognize trillion birds
Fossils stir. Where is
The glacier to which my husband refers?

Shorelines erode.
He is balding but only a little
Lines of red sandbars recede
    & cranes do that mating flight
  Globally
Acknowledged
As true.

Graffiti

We lean back
Into debris fire gutted kitchen walls
 A house a
River a dock we
Glimpsed from
The beltway. A Roman numeral
    Clock between us.

        1.   We smoke blow smoke rings
Watch graffiti shift morph

The tongue an instrument of curled
    Split hollows.

        -        We lean
Eucalyptus & our headstrong natures
Eclipse the sweet
A genetic intensity. Sheer pink

        Spaceships are captured
In this river see
        the balloon resistance
Parachutes torn by rock
& they who don't know
What reality is. Individual.
    Not Roswell but a watery
Reflection

The fire gutted houses by rivers &
Graffiti
  We scribed by crayon
The evidence
 In pebble & spilled blue rune
Our mutual exile.

(This is where the poets play)

Binding (The Asteroid Rose

Worn glue & thin thread
Where did the little prince depart
    Antoinette?

Misplaced garden
    Hard bound paperback
Somebody euthanized // voice
    strings cut

Cockroaches feed upon
    riddlers
      arrogance of time

They are
    Inferno so ancient
  Ring on ring
Quality of death
Ribcage canary
When the lantern of relocation
Is stripped away

Witness is witness

I cannot see the angles of your bedroom
    The hollowed echo of your loss
In shelter
Who sleeps with who

Plastic sextoys or flesh
What made you barren // do you feel barren

Horse head in the bed?
Was that Mary of Fatima
Met us at the door
Accountant
Notebook in hand.

Do not kill
She said.
The asteroid rose is dead

Witness is

Cockroaches scurry
Into the pink pink ceramic
Dish
It once fed
Antoinette's rose
Once wound only
A deviant clown's incarnation.

Before

the tower fell
A Ukrainian man saw himself called
Nazi a perpetrator of genocide

After

cow teat rip
In the calf's pink
Mouth
　At the stroke
Clock
Bell
　　　Meteor.
But the calf tears by chance
Is torn away
　By machine so milk occurs.

Easier to believe when it happens to somebody else.
She knew, who, the
Sentient being
　A lamb bleating
Into the mouth of the machine

Before the blackout
When the wind had a name
& the vastness tolled
Someone heard
& was informed
That their experience did not occur

　The kiss through wire.

What is innocence? —: that. & quick quick

      children changed

To the cloth grin rot

Dolls incur

        When rot landfills

        Make landfall

Lee Said To Me

I would give my life to anyone. Mania &
Depression keep me
Back

        &

took a bus

I took a grey bus
Into the hollowed out forest
Of suicides
  Rang for the stop but changed my mind
The hanged man spinning
Ruby slippers clicking
      I stepped back upon the bus
When the bus came by
Left the forest of suicides
  But have returned. I'd give my life for you I'd give
the world for you
Ballet on the stage take to the streets
Grenade pins like thorn
Pulled then spat to rattle

Glacial Air Pockets Opening

Maybe

This house is haunted
Maybe the world is haunted too —: years
Back
    Nearly an eon

The glacial air pockets shifted &

A girl called Heather
Dark arts practiced
Torched sacs of arachnid babies webbed
    Safe in a ceiling corner
As she urged my child do the same.

Torch the spiders
Grind insect & annelid to gravel
& spit phlegm as signature.

These mentors
Beauty suiting the creature of lies
      These monsters

Are not papier-mâché
Piñatas —: spectral unicorns
Stuffed with Mardi Gras baubles
& false pearls

The room is haunted
The world is
Haunted
But the dogs call out the demons
Sweetheart
Shadow puppetries do not guide our hand
Lizzie Lizzie Lizzie

Borden
Darkness be damned.

From What Tree

Plums
The cadence of peace
Plum trees. Flowering white?
I've never seen one.

   Index & thumb tear at the petals.
   From the corner
White of the solar eye
A combat primitive &
Without windows
        The streak a street cat's
        tear. Nearly cheetah — purple

Plums. A mirage only
To the extinct. An illusion
Optical—: a mauve elephant
   Or a young woman
Her bonnet tied under the chin? Age 8

   My child drew
Crayon gold & green
A mother cheetah sleek
Sliding through the hourglass

        Side to side
        Her baby
& in stride they held their own -/:
Solidarity amidst the leaves.
No

Wicks, Shifting // As He Speaks

It's hard to not take it personally
That far bend in the river

Bundles of bread & blankets left
There for the friends

The wick of a candle shifting
Like lace in the wind

Fear can be a place of consolation
Knees tucked to the chin

Nearly fetal
Feeling the human crease between

Your own ribs
The present rib the missing rib

The fire invents itself
Over & over again

Moonlight traces the bundles
Waiting in the river niche

We will never he says to the world
Never run out of love & respect

The most necessary freedoms
An uncensored moonlit blood

Moon hallow's Eve ghost
   Montage lingering

Tongue cut
On barbed wire

Russian troops withdraw from Bucha; Civilian bodies,
atrocities, disclosed. Russia denies accountability.
April 3, 2022

Catching the Milky Way:
The liberation of Kherson, 11/11/22
(For Eva)

It was dinner time, the 4 cats mewing about her ankles.
They had eaten cornbread & honey,
meat, she scraped scraps into 4 small blue bowls.
It it clear? She asked her dad.
He looked through the skylight, a web of tree
twigs , branches, too damp now for
kindling. Forgot the moon was climbing
tonight he said. His hands were full
of suds, a cup unwashed on the counter.
She said hey dad, says they took back a city:
they saw gutted landscape rife with
homecomings. Men women children
carried flowers, touched lightly as
leaves, laughing. Some glimpse on
parameters of conflict, receding.
The evening news ended past denouement
& the young girl — 15, 16 Years of age —:
zipped her blue jacket, pushed her wire rim glasses
farther toward the bridge of her nose —:
called over her shoulder hey Dad I'm going
to catch the Milky Way, I grabbed the camera.
The door clicked & although the moon disrupted the shine.
There was still shine, pattern, paradigm. & the girl
caught The Milky Way her arms flash blue as a star too —
something — trailed down pale green
falling until it could be seen no more.

Carolyn Srygley-Moore (C Leigh Srygley aka) is a resident of Upstate New York with her husband and many animal rescues. She's a graduate of Johns Hopkins University where she won awards; has been privileged to study, via Albany's New York Writer's Institute, with the Irish poet John Montagu (RIP). She has worked with Real Stories Gallery, writing on various cultural-pathologies like Trafficking. She has been Published by *I am not a silent poet*, among many other journals; in the last 13 years has been nominated for 2 Pushcarts and one Best-of-the-Web. She's authored books and chapbooks, most notably *Ode to Horatio and Other Saviors* (Crisis Chronicles Press) and *Miracles Of the Blog;* a series (Punk Hostage Press). No portions of this Book have been published elsewhere due to the nature of Putin's invasion of The Ukraine, the sense that the Book has just begun.

BLACK DRAGON POETRY SOCIETY

CERTIFIED AND APPROVED